Consulting Authors

Barbara Coulter, Frankie Dungan, Joseph B. Rubin,
Carl B. Smith, Shirley Wright

Contributors

The Princeton Review, Time Magazine

The Princeton Review is not
affiliated with Princeton
University or ETS.

McGraw-Hill School Division

A Division of The McGraw·Hill Companies

McGraw-Hill School Division
Two Penn Plaza
New York, New York 10121

Printed in the United States of America

ISBN 0-02-184721-5/1, Book 5

2 3 4 5 6 7 8 9   043/071   04 03 02 01 00

Macmillan/McGraw-Hill Edition

McGRAW-HILL READING

Authors

James Flood

Jan E. Hasbrouck

James V. Hoffman

Diane Lapp

Angela Shelf Medearis

Scott Paris

Steven Stahl

Josefina Villamil Tinajero

Karen D. Wood

McGraw-Hill
School Division

New York   Farmington

UNIT 1

THINK ABOUT IT!

Many Paths

8

Peck

   peck

      peck

on the warm brown egg.

OUT comes a neck
OUT comes a leg.

How

   does

      a chick

who's not been about,

discover the trick

of how to get out?

by Aileen Fisher

9

Hide-and-Seek

A dog and some sheep play hide-and-seek.
One, two, three! Dog needs to peek.
He looks around! He cannot see:

Eight sheep feet up in the tree,
Two sheep sailing in the creek,
One sheep down under the street,
Two sheep kneeling next to the queen.

Dog cannot see them.
What a bind!
Seven sheep too hard to find.

Meet

Joyce Dunbar was a teacher for many years until she became deaf. Then she turned to writing. "I like to write in the mornings and spend the afternoons gardening," she says. When she is not writing, she thinks about writing. Dunbar says she even thinks about writing in her sleep!

Meet

Chris Downing loves to draw and paint animals. He was happy when Joyce Dunbar asked him to illustrate *Seven Sillies*. "I am very proud of *Seven Sillies*. I hope that all children will enjoy it," he says.

Seven Sillies

by Joyce Dunbar
illustrated by Chris Downing

On a bright and shining morning,
Pig looked into the pond.

And Pig called over to Sheep.

"What do you see in the pond?" asked Pig.
"I see a pig and a sheep," answered Sheep.
"Such a beautiful sheep!"

And Sheep called over to Goat.

"What do you see in the pond?" asked Sheep.

"I see a pig and a sheep and a goat," answered Goat.

"Such a gorgeous goat."

And Goat called over to Rabbit.

"What do you see in the pond?" asked Goat.
"I see a pig and a sheep and a goat
and a rabbit," answered Rabbit.
"Such a splendid rabbit!"

And Rabbit called over to Hen.

"What do you see in the pond?"
asked Rabbit.
"I see a pig and a sheep and a goat and
a rabbit and a hen," said Hen.
"Such a fine, feathered hen."

And Hen called over to Mouse.

"What do you see in the pond?" asked Hen.
"I see a pig and a sheep and a goat and a
rabbit and a hen and a mouse," said Mouse.
"Such a dear, little mouse."

And Mouse called over to Frog.

"What do you see in the pond?"
asked Mouse.

"I see seven sillies," answered Frog.

"Seven sillies?" asked the pig and the sheep and the goat and the rabbit and the hen and the mouse. "What do you mean?"

"They are all in the pond and they want to get out," said Frog.

"How can we get them out?"

"You will have to jump in and fetch them,"
answered Frog.

So the pig and the sheep and the goat and the rabbit and the hen and the mouse all jumped into the water with a *splash!*

"There is nothing in the pond, after all!"
they said.

"Oh, yes, there is," laughed Frog.
"There is a handsome pig,
a beautiful sheep,
a gorgeous goat,

a splendid rabbit,
a fine, feathered hen,
a dear, little mouse,
and that makes seven sillies."

The animals scrambled out of the pond all sopping and dripping with water. They did feel very silly!

Then . . .

"How many sillies?" asked Pig.

"Seven," said Frog.

Pig began to count.

The other animals joined in.

"One, two, three, four, five, six—"
The only one left was Frog.
"Aha!" they laughed. "SEVEN SILLIES!"

"We see a frog that can't count," they said.

"Such a silly frog!"

Story Questions & Activities

1. What did Goat see in the pond?

2. What were the animals really seeing?

3. What will Hen see the next time she looks in the pond?

4. Is "Seven Sillies" a good title? Why?

5. What kind of stunt might the seven sillies do?

Write Another Seven Sillies Story

Think of seven silly things.
Write a story about them.
Draw a picture to go with
your story.

I have seven silly tops.

Make a Number Collage

Look in old magazines.
Find number words.
Cut them out.
What design will you make?
Paste them on paper.

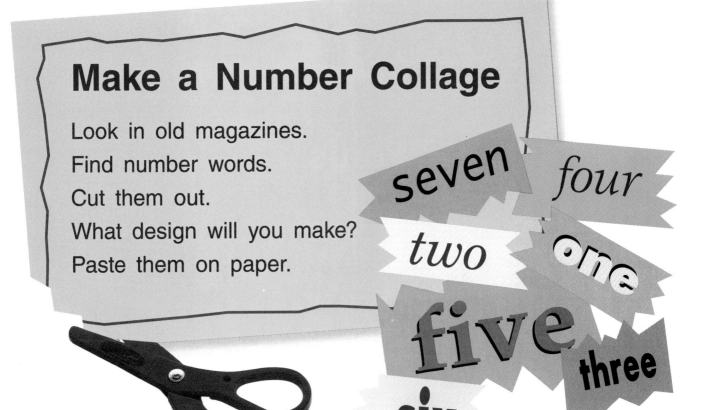

Find Out More

Find out more about life in a pond.
What plants and animals live there?

Dictionary Words

word   meaning

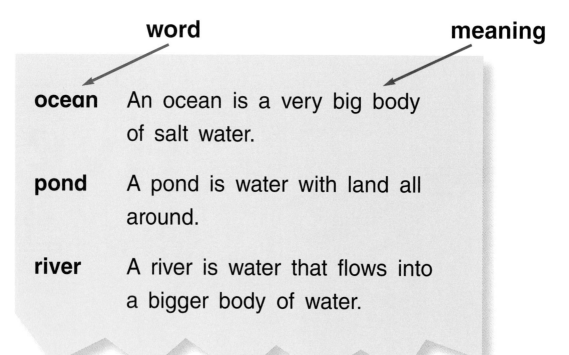

ocean   An ocean is a very big body
of salt water.

pond   A pond is water with land all
around.

river   A river is water that flows into
a bigger body of water.

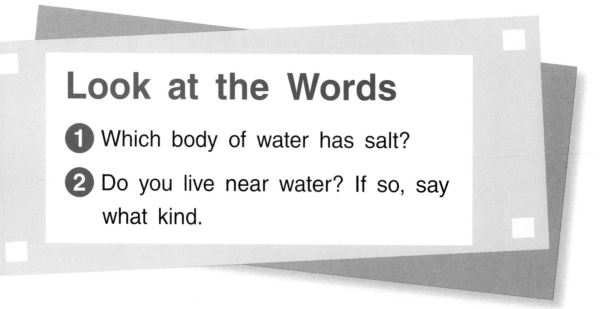

Look at the Words

1 Which body of water has salt?

2 Do you live near water? If so, say
what kind.

Salsa

Jenny made salsa.

This is the recipe that she followed:

   3 chopped ripe tomatoes
   1 chopped large onion
   1 cup lemon juice
   1 chopped clove of garlic

Put all of these things into a bowl.
Mix them well. Add salt and black pepper.

Jenny followed the directions.
Soon, the salsa was ready.
She put it on the table with some chips.

To help answer the question, ask yourself: "What would I do next?"

What will happen next?
○ Jenny will eat the salsa.
○ Jenny will put the onion in the bowl.

The Peach

A field mouse in pink sneakers
   is trying to reach
The peach in the sky
That he has seen from the beach.
That sweet little field mouse!
He runs a blue streak,
Up, up, up the steep trail of the peak.
As he reaches the top,
The peach falls in the sea.
"No fair!" squeaks the field mouse,
"That peach was for me!"

Meet Pat Hutchins

Pat Hutchins spent most of the time outdoors when she was a little girl living in the countryside in England. She loved to explore the fields and woods that were filled with animals and birds. When Hutchins was not exploring, she was drawing. When she grew up she became an illustrator of children's books. Then she started to write books, too. Many of her books are filled with the birds and animals that she loved to watch as a little girl.

48

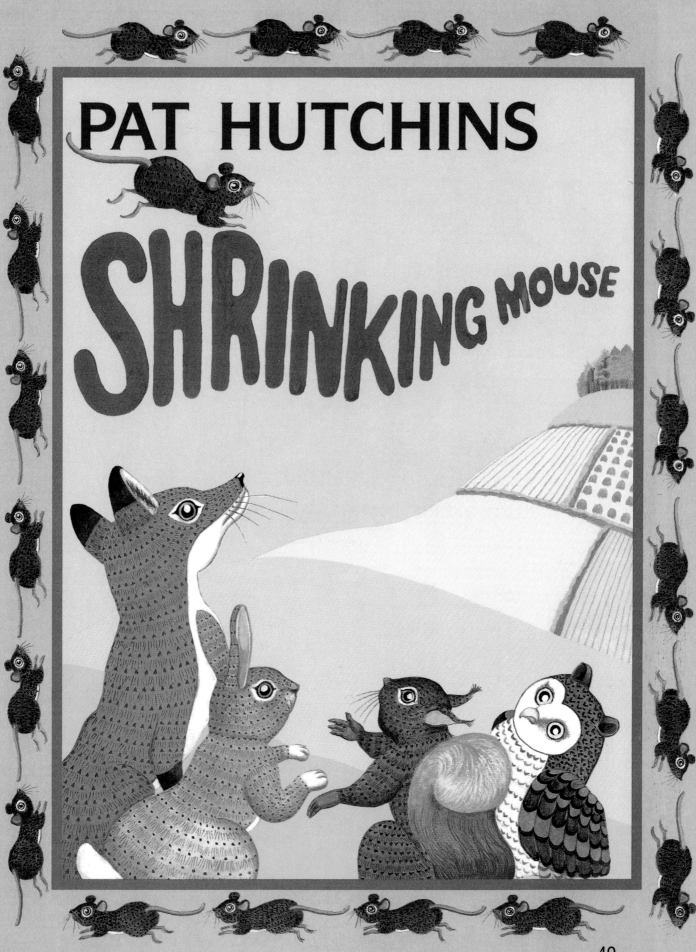

PAT HUTCHINS

SHRINKING MOUSE

Fox, Rabbit, Squirrel, and Mouse were sitting at the edge of their wood, looking across the fields. "Look at that tiny wood over there," said Mouse. "It's even smaller than I am. And look, there's Owl flying toward it."

"Oh, dear!" said Fox. "He's shrinking.
I'll go and tell him to come back
before he disappears altogether."
And Fox set out after Owl.

"Oh, dear!" cried Rabbit. "Fox is shrinking, too. I'll go and tell him to come back before he disappears like Owl!"

And Rabbit set off after Fox.

"Oh, dear!" cried Squirrel.
"Rabbit is shrinking, too!
I'll go and tell him to come back
before he disappears like Fox!"
And Squirrel set off after Rabbit.

Poor Mouse was very upset.
"Squirrel is shrinking, as well!" he
thought. "I must try and stop him
before he disappears like the rest
of my friends."
And Mouse scampered after Squirrel.

"The wood is getting bigger," thought
Mouse. "I must be shrinking, too!"
Poor Mouse didn't want to be any
smaller, but he kept on running.

"The wood is really big now," thought Mouse. "I must have nearly disappeared!" Mouse didn't want to disappear, but he kept on running.

And when he got to the wood, there were Owl and all his friends.

"Have I disappeared?" asked Mouse.

"No," they said. "You're just the right size!"

"Good," said Mouse. "Let's go home." But when he turned to look at their wood, it was very, very small.

"Oh," Mouse cried. "Our wood has shrunk, too! We can't go home!"

"Follow me," said Owl.
So they did.

And as they got closer
to their wood, it got bigger . . .

and bigger.

"Are we getting smaller?"
asked Mouse.
"No," said Owl as they reached
their wood. "We're all just the
right size."
And he flew away.

"Oh, dear!" said Fox.

"Owl is shrinking again."

"Don't worry," said Mouse.

"I'm sure he'll be the right size

when he comes back."

And he was.

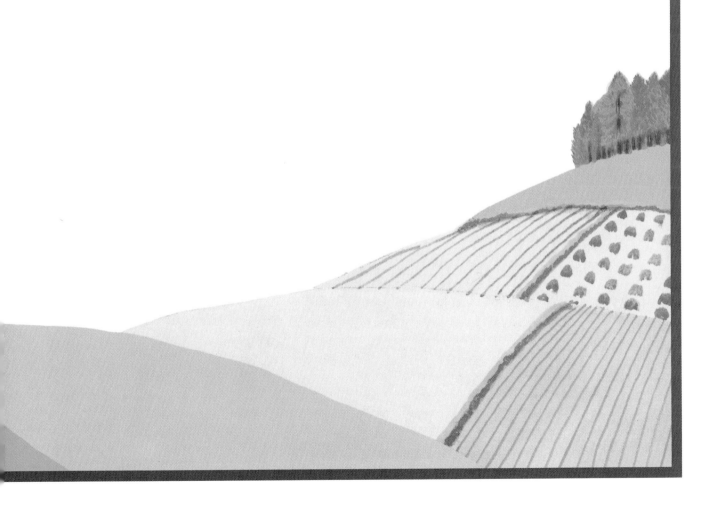

Story Questions & Activities

1. How many animals are in this story?

2. Why did the animals seem smaller?

3. Is our moon as small as it seems?

4. Tell the story in your own words.

5. How is this story like "Seven Sillies"?

Write About a Change in Size

Think of a time you saw something get smaller.
Draw a picture to show it.
Write about it.

The plane went high and got small.

78

Make a Here and There Picture

Draw many trees.

Make some big and some small.

Cut them out and paste them on paper.

Make some trees look close.

Make some trees look far away.

Add some animals and plants to your picture.

Find Out More

There are many kinds of trees.

Find out about trees in the forest.

What are their names?

What do they look like?

Read a Newsletter

Wood Times

March 13, 2005

Mouse Shrinks

by Pam Mack

On Monday, Mouse shrank.
Other animals in the wood are scared.
They do not want to shrink.

Owl said Mouse did not shrink.
Experts are looking into this.

Read the Newsletter

1 What happened to the mouse?

2 When did it happen? Where?

Sally and Her Stick

Sally is a two-year-old dog.
Sally loves to play.
She plays with her stick.
Sally's owner throws her stick.
Sally runs and brings it back.
She plays for many hours.

Sally talks to her stick when
she plays.
"Woof, woof, woof," she barks.
"Grrr, grrr, grrr," she growls.
"Arrr, arrr, arrr," she argues.
Only Sally knows what she is saying.

Reading the story carefully makes the questions easier to answer.

The next time Sally's stick is thrown —
○ she will probably take a nap
○ she will probably run after it

Raindrops

Tonya had to know,
When raindrops fall,
    Where do they go?

She got dressed in her yellow raincoat.
She set out a leaf and hoped it would float.

She poked the leaf boat with her
    big yellow toe,
It went around slowly and then started
    to flow.
She began to feel the rain on her face,
And followed the boat to the raindrop place.

Meet Joanna Cole

Joanna Cole has been writing since she was a little girl. When she grew up, she worked as a teacher, librarian, and editor. Today she is the author of many award-winning children's books. She is especially known for the Magic School Bus books. The main character, Ms. Frizzle, is based on her very own science teacher.

Meet Mavis Smith

Mavis Smith has always liked to draw. She has drawn pictures and written over 50 books for children, including *A Snake Mistake* and *Which Way, Ben Bunny?* She also makes collages that are shown in art shows. She lives in New Hope, Pennsylvania.

You Can't Smell a Flower with Your EAR!

All About Your 5 Senses

by Joanna Cole

illustrated by Mavis Smith

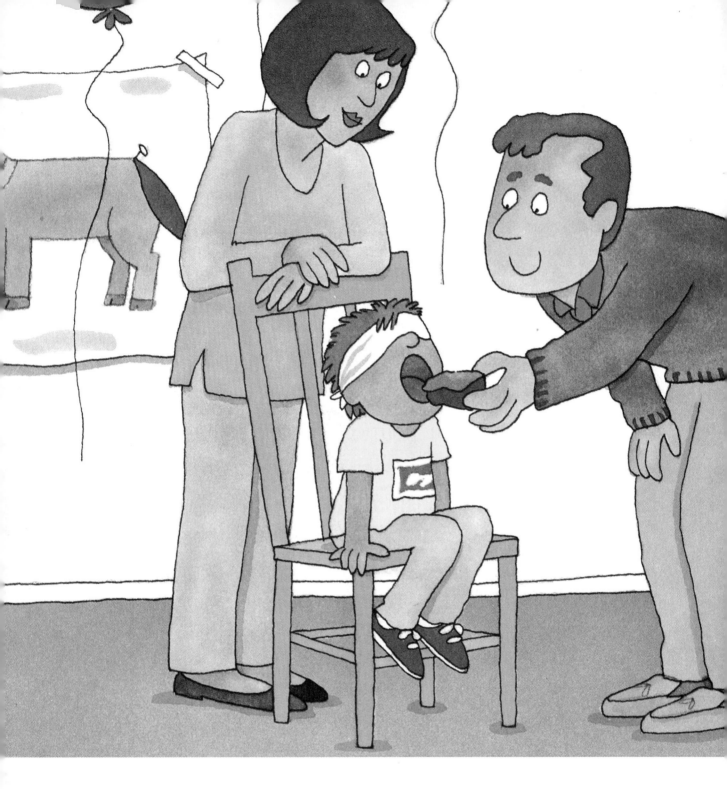

It's your birthday! There's a surprise for you. Your mom puts a blindfold on you. A moment later you smell chocolate. Then something is put in your mouth. You taste sweet cake.

"But that is not the real surprise," says your sister. "Put out your hand," says your dad. You touch something soft. You hear a little mew! Before you pull off the blindfold, you know what you will see.

It's a kitten.

Every day you use your nose to smell, your tongue to taste, your skin to feel, your ears to hear, and your eyes to see.

These are your five sense organs. Each one tells you something different about the world around you. They do this by sending messages to your brain.

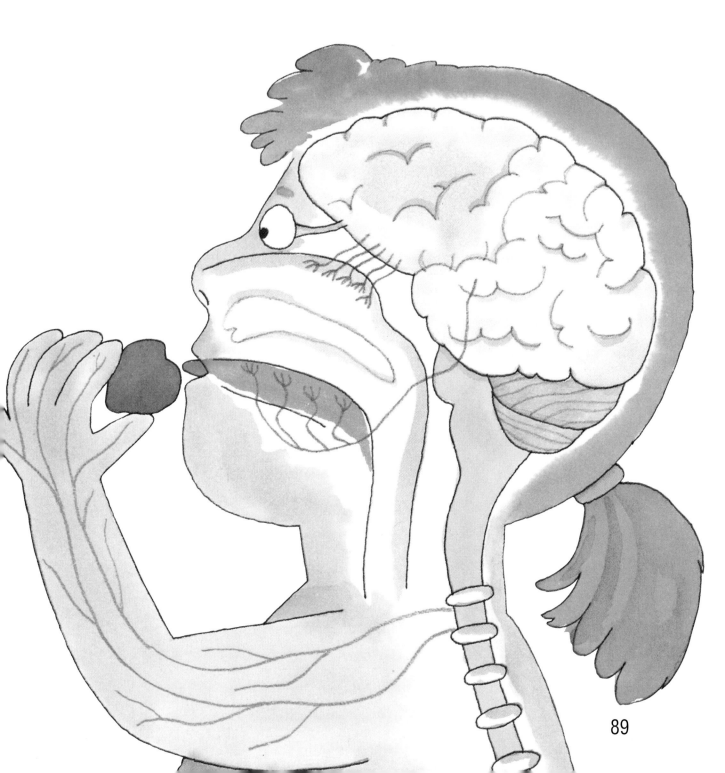

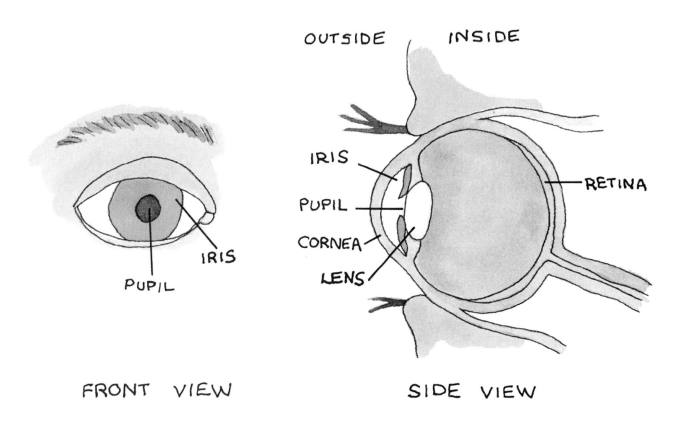

OUTSIDE   INSIDE

IRIS

PUPIL

CORNEA

LENS

RETINA

FRONT VIEW   SIDE VIEW

IRIS

PUPIL

SEEING

Is your eyeball really a ball? Yes! Most of
your eye is hidden inside your skull. Here is
what your whole eye looks like. Each of your
eyes has an opening to let in light. That
opening is called the pupil.

Your eyes are made to see. How do they work?
Look at a hat. Light bounces off the hat and goes
into your eye. The light hits the back of your
eyeball. A picture of the hat is made there.

Nerves—like wires—carry messages about the
picture from the back of your eye to special places
in your brain. You need your brain <u>and</u> your eyes
to see.

Sometimes you can see two pictures in one.

Try This

In this picture, do you see a white vase? Or do you see two black dogs looking at each other? You may see one picture, and then the other. But your brain cannot see both pictures at once.

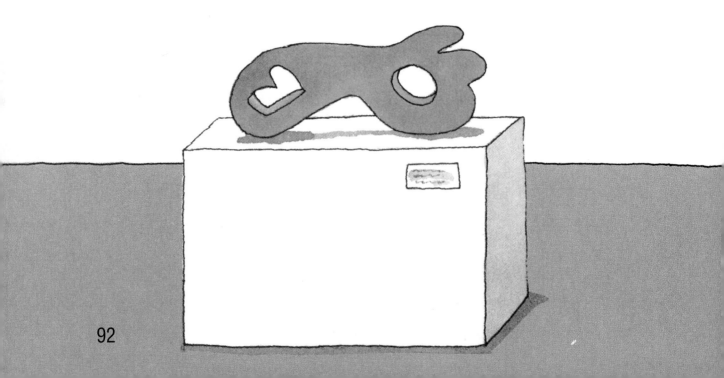

HEARING

You want to fool your friend. You say, "You can't see your ears." "Yes, I can," says your friend. Who is right? You both are! Your friend can see the outside part of her ears.

But she cannot see the other parts. Those are inside her head.

The inside parts are the true, hearing parts of the ear. Your ears pick up sound waves in the air. Sound waves are tiny movements or vibrations.

(You say it like this: vie-BRAY-shuns.) You can hear vibrations.

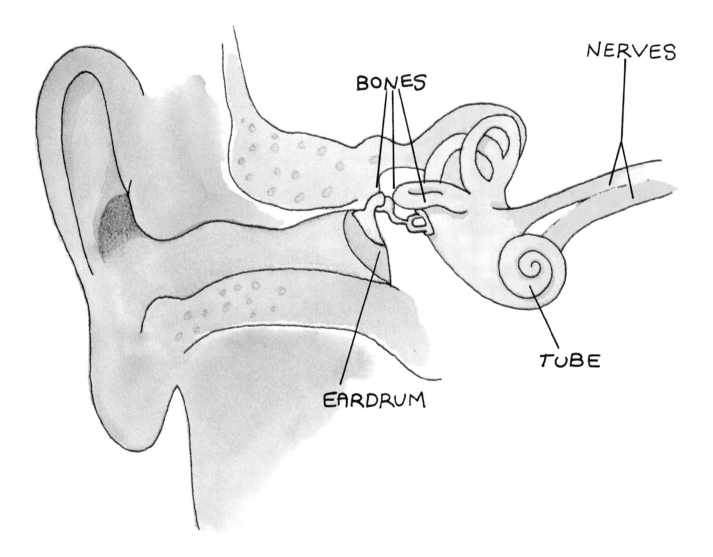

Sound vibrations in the air go into your ear. They hit a stretchy skin—your eardrum.

Then the eardrum vibrates, too. On the other side of the eardrum are three tiny, tiny bones. These bones start to vibrate, too.

Beyond the bones is a tube filled with liquid. The liquid starts to vibrate, too. These vibrations make nerves near the tube send messages to your brain's hearing centers. You need your ears <u>and</u> your brain to hear.

Your ears also tell your brain where a sound is.

Try This

Tell a friend to hide. You
cannot see her. But if she
makes a noise, you know
where to look. That is
because the sound reaches
one ear first. Then it
reaches your other ear.
The difference is very,
very small. But your brain
can tell.

SMELLING

You are walking past a pizza place. There is a hot pizza in the oven. You cannot see the pizza. But your nose tells you it is there! That's because your nose is made for smelling.

How does your nose smell? When the pizza is baking, tiny bits go out of the oven. These bits are called molecules. (You say it like this: MOLL-uh-kewls.) Molecules are so small we cannot see them.

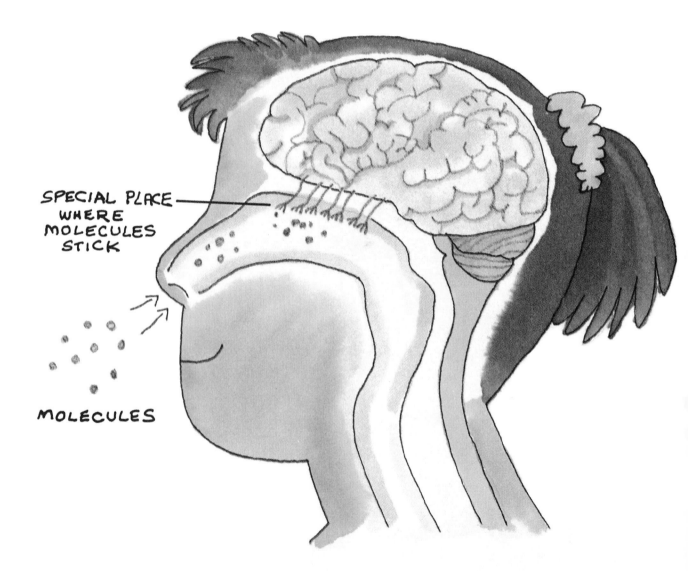

SPECIAL PLACE WHERE MOLECULES STICK

MOLECULES

When you breathe in air, pizza molecules go into your nose. High up in your nose is a special place where molecules can stick. Nearby nerves send messages about the pizza molecules to your brain. Then you smell the pizza.

Try This

Find something that smells good—flowers, soap, apples, or oranges. Go near and breathe the way you usually do. Do you smell the nice smell?

Now put your nose near and <u>sniff</u>. The smell is stronger now. Why?

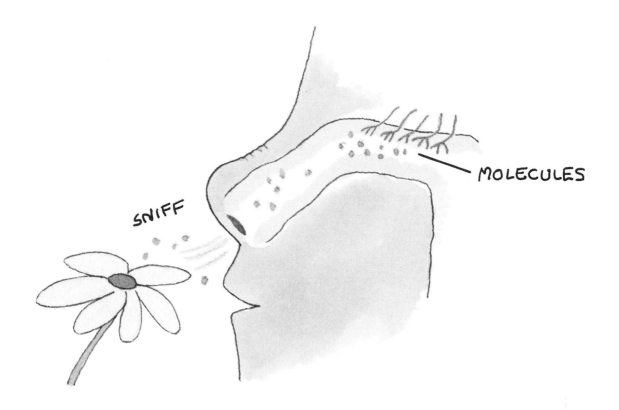

SNIFF

MOLECULES

When you sniff, you pull air straight up your nose. More molecules stick near the nerves, so you get more of the smell.

TASTING

The pizza <u>smells</u> so good, it must <u>taste</u> great, too. Thank goodness you have taste buds on your tongue. Molecules in the food you eat go inside the taste buds. And nerves send taste messages to your brain. Then you taste your food.

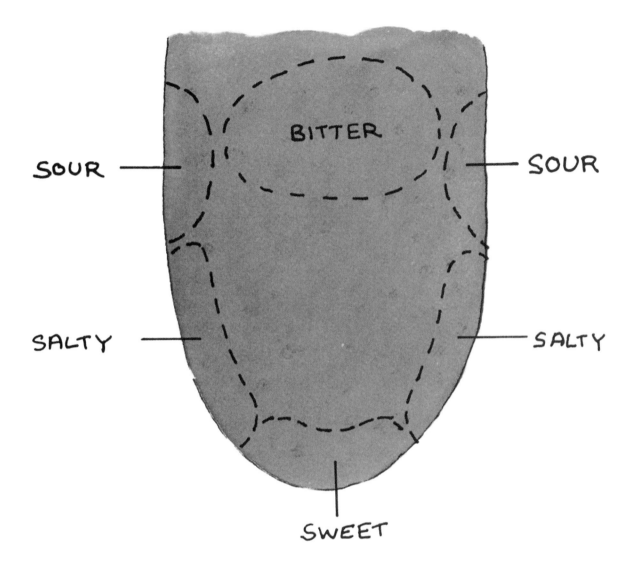

Different parts of your tongue pick up
different tastes. One part of your tongue is
best at tasting sweet things. Another part is
best at tasting salty things. Another part
tastes sour things. And still another part
tastes bitter things.

Your sense of taste gets a lot of help from your sense of smell.

Try This

Get two flavors of ice cream. Ask a friend to close her eyes and hold her nose. Give her a taste of each flavor. Can she tell which is which? Probably not. Then let your friend taste the ice cream <u>without</u> holding her nose. It will be easy to tell the flavors.

FEELING

You have nerves in your skin for touch and pressure, hot and cold, and pain. Just by feeling, you can tell that a pillow is soft,

a rock is hard,

a snowball is cold,

and a potato is hot.

The nerves in your skin tell your brain all kinds
of things. Some parts of your body have more
touch nerves than others.

There are many other ways to test your senses.
See if you can smell when you're breathing <u>out</u>.
Or see bright light with your eyes closed.

Or taste when
you have a cold.

Does something feel
smoother when you rub
it with your arm or
with your fingertips?

You can even try smelling
a flower with your ear.

Good luck!

1. What are the five senses?

2. Why can't you taste food when you have a cold?

3. If food smells bad, what should you do?

4. Tell how each of your senses helps you.

5. Tell how two foods from "The Shopping List" taste.

Write Another Story

You Can't See a Flower with Your Nose! Tell why your nose can't help you see.

My nose can not take pictures.
My eyes can.

114

Play Twenty Questions

Think of an object.
Have classmates ask you questions about how it sounds, smells, tastes, or feels.
You can only answer yes or no.
See how long it takes to get the right answer.

Is it soft?

Does it smell good?

Find Out More

Look at this picture.
Tell what you see.
Find other pictures that trick the eye.

Use a List

A list helps you remember things.

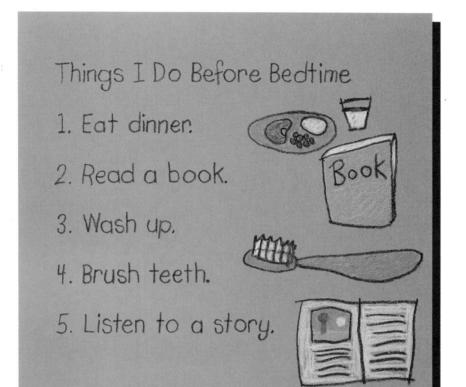

Things I Do Before Bedtime

1. Eat dinner.
2. Read a book.
3. Wash up.
4. Brush teeth.
5. Listen to a story.

Look at the List

❶ Name two things on the list where you use your sense of taste.

❷ What else might you add to the list?

TEST POWER

Who Does the Raccoon Meet?

A raccoon lived by the river.

His name was Poke.

He had a snug nest.

It was made of leaves and grass.

It kept him warm at night.

One day, Poke took a walk by the river.

He saw a very large horse.

Poke asked the horse what his name was.

The horse's name was Polo.

Poke and Polo talked for many hours.

As the sun set, Poke and Polo said good-bye.

What did Poke have at the end of the day?

○ A tummy ache

○ A new friend

Which answer fits the story best?

Kite in the Sky

Would you like to fly
Like a kite in the sky?
You could soar like a bird
And stay up high
In the big, bright, blue sky
To make friends with the moon
And come down by and by.

Meet Arnold Lobel

Arnold Lobel has written and illustrated many award-winning children's books, including the Frog and Toad series. When Lobel was a boy, he loved to read. He would go to the library and check out a big stack of books. Lobel says that writers should write about things they care about. He loves animals and once owned 49 mice. He also had toads and frogs. "I loved those little creatures and I think they led to the creation of my two most famous characters, Frog and Toad."

OWL AND
THE MOON

by Arnold Lobel

One night

Owl went down

to the seashore.

He sat on a large rock

and looked out at the waves.

Everything was dark.

Then a small tip

of the moon

came up

over the edge of the sea.

Owl watched the moon.

It climbed higher and higher

into the sky.

Soon the whole, round moon

was shining.

Owl sat on the rock

and looked up at the moon

for a long time.

"If I am looking

at you, moon,

then you must be

looking back at me.

We must be

very good friends."

The moon did not answer,

but Owl said,

"I will come back

and see you again, moon.

But now I must go home."

Owl walked down the path.

He looked up at the sky.

The moon was still there.

It was following him.

"No, no, moon," said Owl.

"It is kind of you

to light my way.

But you must stay up

over the sea

where you look so fine."

Owl walked on a little farther.

He looked at the sky again.

There was the moon

coming right along with him.

"Dear moon," said Owl,

"you really must not

come home with me.

My house is small.

You would not fit

through the door.

And I have nothing

to give you for supper."

Owl kept on walking.

The moon

sailed after him

over the tops of the trees.

"Moon," said Owl,

"I think that

you do not hear me."

Owl climbed

to the top of a hill.

He shouted

as loudly as he could,

"Good-bye, moon!"

The moon went behind some clouds.

Owl looked and looked.

The moon was gone.

"It is always

a little sad

to say good-bye to a friend,"

said Owl.

Owl came home.

He put on his pajamas

and went to bed.

The room was very dark.

Owl was still feeling sad.

All at once,

Owl's bedroom

was filled with silver light.

Owl looked out of the window.

The moon was coming

from behind the clouds.

"Moon, you have followed me

all the way home.

What a good, round friend

you are!" said Owl.

Then Owl put his head

on the pillow

and closed his eyes.

The moon was shining

down through the window.

Owl did not

feel sad at all.

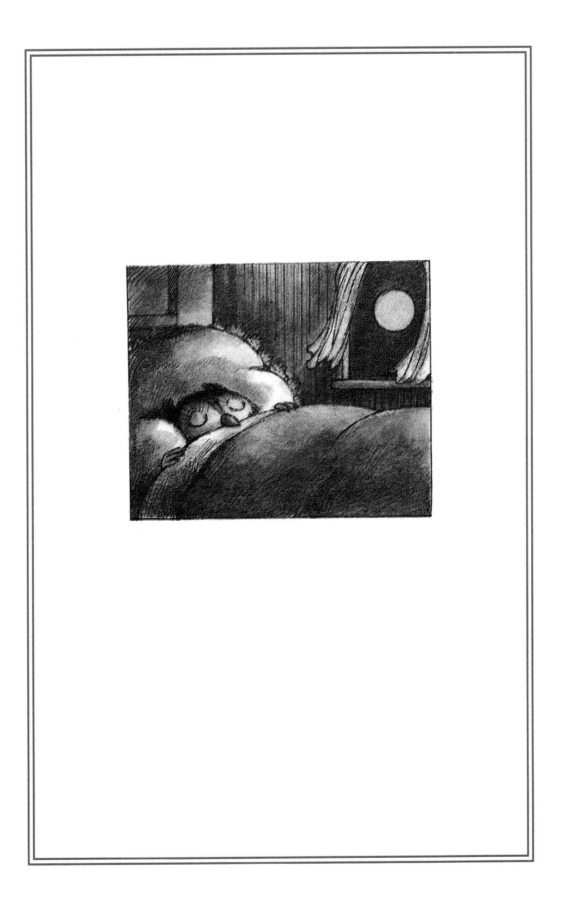

Story Questions & Activities

1. Where does the story take place?

2. Why didn't the moon talk to Owl?

3. Why can't we see the moon sometimes?

4. What is funny about this story?

5. What would the owl from "Shrinking Mouse" say to this owl?

Write a Diary Entry

Pretend you are Owl.
Tell about your night out.
Write it as a diary entry.

Dear Diary,
I saw the moon tonight.
I felt happy.
Owl

138

Draw a Moon Picture

Draw a night picture.
Add a moon to your picture.
Which moon will you show?

Find Out More

Find out why we see only parts of the moon on some nights.

Let's Read Signs

Signs help us stay safe.

Look at the Signs

1 What does the exit sign tell you?

2 Where do you see the stop sign?

Fun in the Sun

The beach is fun.
It is fun to run on the sand.
The waves crash on the shore.
The cold water hits our toes.

Now, the sun is setting in the sky.
The sky is pink, purple, and orange.
The sand is cold.
It is time to go home.

Which answer fits the story best?

Good-bye, sand.
Good-bye, sun.
Good-bye, beach.

In this story, the beach is —
○ a good place to go
○ too cold to visit

At Night

When the moon comes out at night,
Bat and owl take flight.

    Fly low, fly high,
    Fly up in the sky.

When the sun has gone to bed,
Snake pokes out his head.

    Creep fast, creep slow.
    Snake knows where to go.

Look around this night and spy
    for animals that creep and fly!

TIME
FOR KIDS
SPE   RT

The
Night
Animals

When you go to bed, many animals
wake up! They rest when it is daytime
and begin their day at dusk. The night
owl flies around to find something to
eat. Wait! There's a rat. The owl cannot see or
smell the rat. But it can hear the rat. The owl
takes off! Will it get the rat?

145

The bat, too, can use hearing to hunt at night. The bat has wings, but it is not a bird. The bat is the only mammal that can fly.
It looks like a rat with wings. The bat likes to eat bugs.

FIND OUT MORE
Visit our website:
www.mhschool.com/reading

A story from the editors of TIME FOR KIDS.

The sun is too hot for snakes.
They come out in the cool night.

Night animals are all around
us. Not all of them are wild.

Some kinds of pets like to
sleep in the day and come out
at night. The next time you go
to bed, look at your pet. Is
your pet a night animal?

Story Questions & Activities

1. Which of the five senses do the owl and bat use to get their food?

2. How are the owl and bat alike and different?

3. Do you think farmers like bats? Why or why not?

4. Tell about the night animals in your own words.

5. What other night animal stories have you read?

Write a Story

Suppose you are a bat, owl, or snake. Tell a story about what you do at night.

The Raccoon

I am a raccoon. I look for food at night. Sometimes, I look in people's trash cans. I make a big mess when I do this. The trash gets all over the place.

Night Animal Riddle

Make up a riddle about a night animal.
Write your riddle in a class book. Here
is a riddle to get you started:

I have wings and
I can fly.
I am a mammal,
not a bird.
What am I?

Find Out More

Choose a night animal you want to
learn more about.
Find out where it lives and what it eats.

Dictionary

A dictionary tells us what words mean.

bat A **bat** is a small mammal that sleeps during the day and flies around at night.

owl An **owl** is a bird that flies and hunts at night.

snake A **snake** is a long, thin animal with scales and no legs.

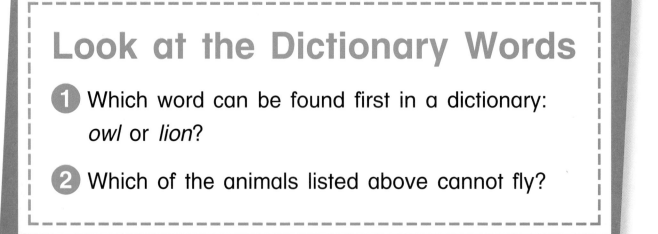

Look at the Dictionary Words

1 Which word can be found first in a dictionary: *owl* or *lion*?

2 Which of the animals listed above cannot fly?

Listen to the Water

Many years ago, an owl lived in a tree.

He was a wise and very old owl.

He had lived for more than a thousand years.

All of the other animals came from near and far
to ask the owl questions.

"Look at the trees," he told the animals. "See how
they move."

"Listen to the river," he told them. "Listen to it flow
over the rocks."

The animals followed the owl's
words and looked at the trees.

They listened to the water.

They found the answers to their questions.

What a wise old owl he must have been!

Think about the story as you read it.

How do you know that this story is
make-believe?

○ Owls do not speak.

○ Water does not flow over rocks.

LONDON BRIDGE

London Bridge is falling down,
falling down, falling down.
London Bridge is falling down,
My fair lady.

Build it up with iron bars,
iron bars, iron bars,
Build it up with iron bars,
My fair lady.

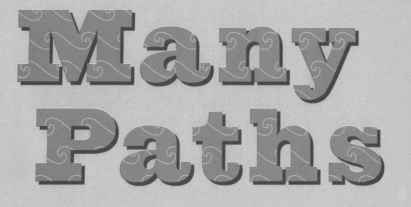

SOLUTION

When I went out to play
   The day had just begun.
"Put on your coat," said the wind.
   "Take off your coat," said the sun.

Now who was in the right?
   And which advice was better?
I solved the problem for myself—
   I just put on my sweater.

by Leland B. Jacobs

156

Little Bear's Tooth

Little Brown Bear had a loose tooth.
So he got a balloon at a red balloon booth.
He tied the balloon string tight to the tooth,
And sat on the stoop till he saw a gray goose.

"Yoo, hoo! Gray Goose!
Can you tug the balloon?
Yoo, hoo! Gray Goose!
Can you take out my tooth?"

So Goose swooped and swooped,
And out came Bear's tooth!

Meet
Harry Horse

Harry Horse is a writer and illustrator. *A Friend for Little Bear* is his first picture book. "*A Friend for Little Bear* has been inside of me for a long time," he says. "It is based on my 3-year-old nephew, Louis. The lesson that Little Bear learns is one we all learn again and again throughout life."

A
Friend
for Little
Bear
by
Harry Horse

Little Bear lived all alone on a desert island.
"I wish I had something to play with," he said.

A stick came floating by. Little Bear picked it out
of the sea. He drew a picture in the sand.
Then he drew some more.
"I need something else to play with," he said.

He was tired of drawing pictures.

A bottle came floating by.
Little Bear picked it out of the sea.

He filled it up with water,
then poured out the water
on the sand.

"I need a cup," said Little Bear,
"to pour the water into."

Then something spotted
came floating by. Little Bear
wondered what it was.

"It isn't a cup," he said,
but he pulled it out
of the sea anyway.

It was a wooden horse.

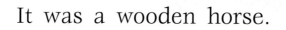

The wooden horse ran around
the island. Little Bear ran after him.

The wooden horse hid. Little Bear
looked for him. They had a lovely time.

They drew pictures in the sand
and filled the bottle again and again.

They played all day long and then
went to sleep under the tall palm tree.

Little Bear woke up.
He rubbed his eyes.

"Look!" he cried. "Lots of things
floating in the water!"

He reached out with his stick and
pulled in as many as he could.

"I don't know what these things are,"
he said, "but I need them, all the same."

He piled them into a heap.
Then he sighed. "I still
do wish I had a cup."

There wasn't much room on the island now. Little Bear had filled it up.

He told the wooden horse to get out of the way.

"Climb onto that," said Little Bear. "I need more room for these boxes."

"Look!" cried Little Bear.

"A cup!"

SNAP!

The roof broke. The wooden horse fell into the sea and floated away.

Little Bear was filling his bottle with water and pouring the water into his cup.

"Watch me!" he cried.
He filled up the bottle again.
"Watch me!" But no one was
there.

He looked up.

He put the bottle down.

He walked all around the island.

"Where are you?" he called.
"I need you!" But no one answered.

"I need my *friend*," said Little Bear.
"I don't need that cup!"

He threw all his things back into the sea and they floated away.

He sat underneath the tall palm tree
and began to cry.

Little Bear dried his eyes.
Then he rubbed them. Something
spotted was floating by. He ran
and pulled it out of the sea.

"I only need you, Wooden Horse,"
he said, and the two of them
danced for joy on the sand.

Story Questions & Activities

1. Where did Little Bear first see the wooden horse?

2. Why did Little Bear want a friend?

3. Where do you think all the things came from?

4. What did Little Bear learn?

5. What other stories have you read about friends?

Write About a Good Friend

Do you have a special toy or teddy bear?
Do you have a friend you like to play with?
Write about a good friend.
Tell what you do together.

I like to play ball with my friend.

Make Something New

Use paper towel rolls.
Use boxes and small pieces of wood.
Use old buttons or beads.
Make something new.

Find Out More

Find out more about islands.
What are they?
Are there any near where
you live?

The Reading Area

People read all kinds of books at the library.

They also read magazines and listen to stories on tape.

Look at the Diagram

1 Where would you sit to listen to a tape?

2 Where are the magazines?

Bob's Cake

Bob the cook is making a cake.
First, he reads his cookbook.
Then, he mixes up the ingredients.
Now, he pops it into the oven to bake.

Bob takes the cake out of the oven.
It is hot. He puts it on the table to cool.

After a few hours, Bob can eat his cake.
It is cool now.
Suddenly, the cake jumps off the plate.
"Sorry, Bob," the cake says.
"I'm not ready to be eaten yet."

Ask yourself: "Why is this story make-believe?"

We know that this story is
make-believe because —
○ there are no bakers named Bob
○ cakes can't talk

What Can Be In It ?

A carton for me! What can be in it?

Can it be a scarf or a jar full of toy cars?

Can it be puzzle parts or
glow-in-the-dark stars?

What kind of surprise can it be?

Whatever it is, it is just for me.

The hard part is waiting to see!

The hard part is waiting to see!

Meet **Johanna Hurwitz**

When Johanna Hurwitz was ten, she wanted to work in a library. But her first love was always writing. Today she has written many books for children. Some of them are funny. "Even my cats and their fleas have made it into a book," Hurwitz says.

Meet **Jerry Pinkney**

As a young boy, Jerry Pinkney liked to draw. Some of his books are about African Americans. Pinkney has also worked on books about Hispanics and Native Americans. Many of his books have won awards.

New Shoes for
Silvia

written by Johanna Hurwitz
illustrated by Jerry Pinkney

196

Once, far away in another America, a package arrived at the post office. The package came from Tía Rosita. Inside there were gifts for the whole family.

For Silvia there was a wonderful present—a pair of
bright red shoes with little buckles that shone in
the sun like silver.

Right away, Silvia took off her old shoes and put on
the beautiful new ones. Then she walked around so
everyone could see.

"Mira, mira," she called. "Look, look."

"Those shoes are as red as the setting sun," her grandmother said. "But they are too big for you."

"Your shoes are as red as the inside of a watermelon," said Papa. "But they are too big. You will fall if you wear them."

"Tía Rosita has sent you shoes the color of a rose," said Mama. "We will put them away until they fit you."

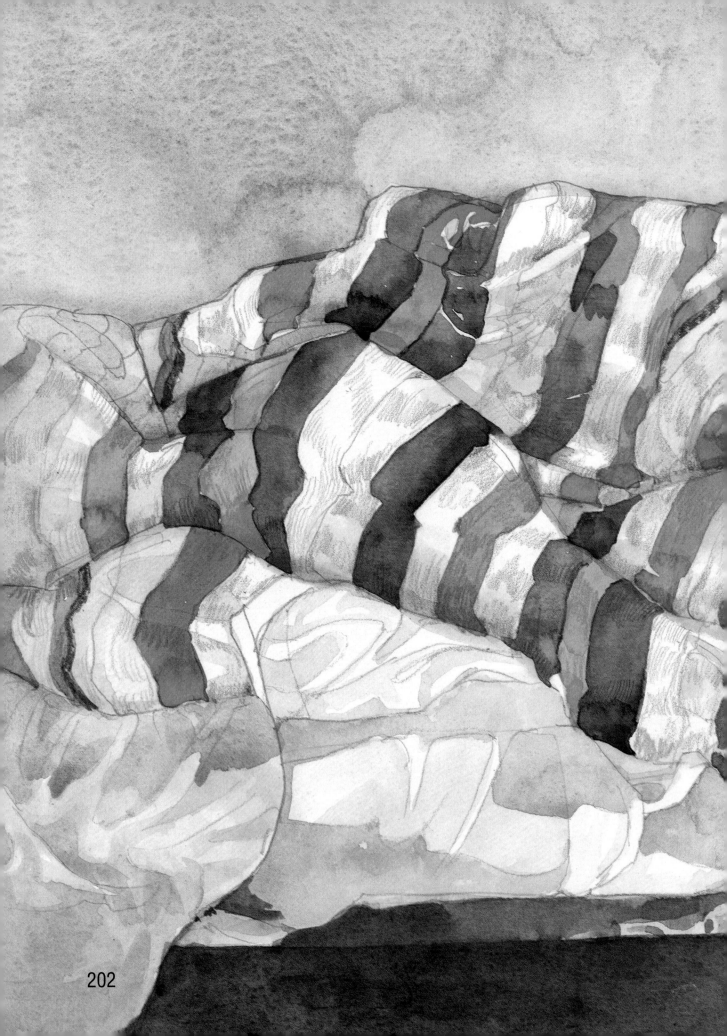

Silvia was sad. What good were new shoes if she couldn't wear them?

That night she slept with them in her bed.

The next morning Silvia put on the red shoes again. Perhaps she had grown during the night.

No. The shoes were still too big. But she saw that they were just the right size to make beds for two of her dolls. Even though it was morning, the dolls went right to sleep in their new red beds.

A week passed, and Silvia tried on the red shoes again. Perhaps she had grown during the week.

No. The shoes were still too big. But she saw that they made a fine two-car train. She pushed them all around the floor. What a good ride the babies had in their red train!

207

Another week passed, and Silvia tried on the red shoes again. Certainly by now she had grown big enough so they would fit.

No. The shoes were still too big. But Silvia found some string and tied it to the shoes. Then she pulled the shoes like oxen working in the field.

Still another week passed, and Silvia tried on the red shoes again. Would they fit now?

No. The shoes were still too big. But she saw that they were just the right size to hold the pretty shells and smooth pebbles that she had collected when she went to the beach with her grandparents.

Another week passed, and another and another. Sometimes Silvia was so busy playing with the other children or helping her mama with the

new baby or feeding the chickens or looking for their eggs that she forgot to try on her new red shoes.

One day Mama wrote a letter to Tía Rosita. Silvia thought about the red shoes. She emptied out all the shells and pebbles and dusted the shoes off on her skirt. They were as red and beautiful as ever. Would they fit today?

Yes.

"Mira, mira," she cried, running to show Mama and the baby. "Look, look. My shoes are not too big now."

Silvia wore her new red shoes when she walked to the post office with Mama to mail the letter.

"Maybe there will be a new package for us," said Silvia.

"Packages don't come every day," said Mama.

"Maybe next time Tía Rosita will send me new blue shoes," said Silvia.

They mailed the letter and walked home. Silvia's shoes were as red as the setting sun. They were as red as the inside of a watermelon. They were as red as a rose. The buckles shone in the sun like silver.

And best of all, the shoes were just the right size for Silvia.

Story Questions & Activities

1 Why couldn't Silvia wear her new shoes?

2 What is the weather like where Silvia lives?

3 What might Silvia do with her shoes when she grows out of them?

4 List the things that Silvia did with her shoes before she could wear them.

5 Have you read stories that take place far away?

My yellow sneakers are the best. They have stars on them.

Use Colorful Words

Think about your favorite pair of shoes.
Draw a picture of them.
Tell what your shoes look like and what color they are.

Make Something with a Shoe Box

Use a shoe box.
Create a scene from the story.
Use markers, paper,
and magazines.

Find Out More

Find out more about
the post office.
Learn about
different stamps.

The Library

You can take library books and tapes home.
But then you must return them.

librarian

desk

Look at the Diagram

1 Where would you go to return a book?

2 If you needed help, who would you ask?

Raking Leaves

Winter is coming soon.

The trees are losing their leaves.

They are landing on the garden.

We will have to rake them up.

We can make a leaf pile.

Maybe we can jump in the pile.

Soon, the snow will come.

It will cover our leaf pile.

It will cover the garden.

We can shovel it into a pile.

Maybe we can jump in that pile, too.

A FACT is something that is true.

Which is a FACT from this story?

○ The leaves are falling.

○ Summer is coming soon.

First Flight

On her first flight, a bird flaps her wings.
She flaps and flaps and up she flies.
She goes higher and higher, up in the sky.
The baby birds ask, "Where is she now?
Has she learned to fly? Can she show
    us how?
Is she hurt? Is she safe?"
    The birds turn around.
They see her landing at home safe
    and sound.

Meet Tomek Bogacki

Tomek Bogacki was born in Poland and lives there now. In school he studied art, and when he finished, he began to illustrate children's books. When Bogacki draws pictures for a book, he often goes to an old farm house deep in the woods where it is very quiet. This way he can pay attention to his work.

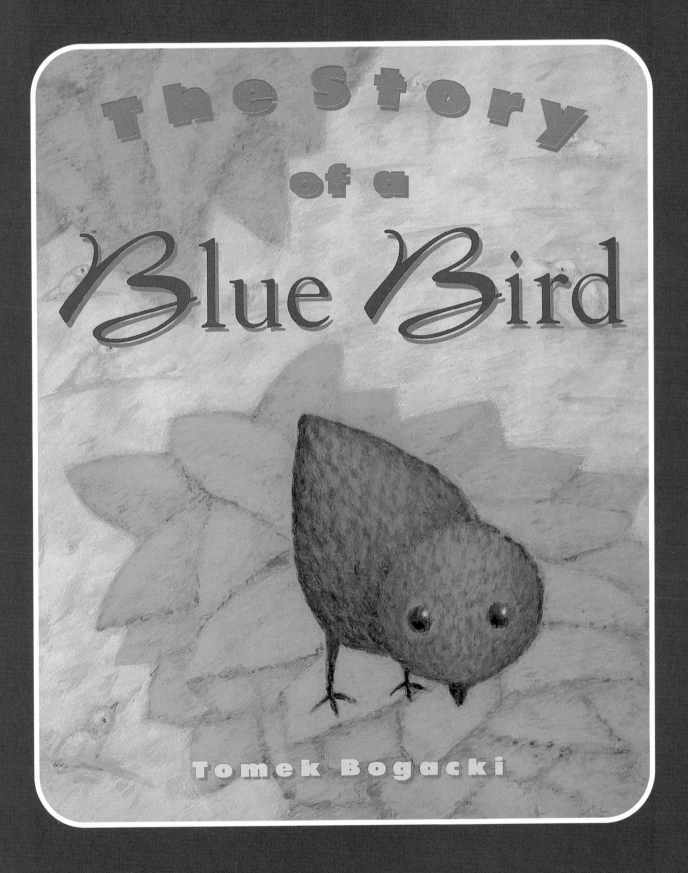

The Story of a
Blue Bird

Tomek Bogacki

A little blue bird was born
in the nest of a big tree.
He grew fast.

"Why don't you go and learn how to fly with your brother and sister? Don't you wonder what is out there?" his mother asked.

"Oh, yes. But I am still a little bit afraid," the blue bird answered.

So while the other birds tested their wings the little blue bird sat in the nest, watching.

At night he couldn't sleep, imagining what might be out there beyond the trees.

"Mama, Mama, what is out there?" he asked.
"Nothing," she said. "Now go to sleep."

Nothing? he wondered ...
And he couldn't stop thinking about it.

The next morning the little
blue bird was gone, and
everyone wondered what
had happened.

"Nothing, nothing, where is this nothing?" the little blue bird thought as he walked away from his nest in the big tree.

"Is nothing high, or is nothing low?
Is nothing here, or is nothing there?
What does nothing look like?"

There was no one to ask, so he kept on going.

239

He came upon a pool of blue water. It looked like nothing he had ever seen before, but he didn't know if this was the nothing he was looking for.

"What are you looking for?" someone asked him.

241

"Nothing," he answered,
surprised.
"Oh! Come with me," said
the green bird.

And the blue bird joined
him.

Suddenly a flock of colorful
birds came flying by.

"What are you looking for?"
they asked.
"Nothing," the green bird
answered.
"Oh! Come with us," they
called.

And the green bird spread
his wings and flew up.

And the little blue bird
forgot that he was afraid
of flying. He, too, spread
his wings and flew up to
join them.

And they flew high, and
they flew low. They flew
here, and they flew there.

"How wonderful it is to fly,"
the little blue bird thought.

"Where have you been?
What have you seen?"
asked his brother and sister
when the blue bird came
back home.
"What happened to make
you fly so well?" asked his
mother.

"Nothing," said the blue
bird, happily fluttering his
wings.

248

"Tell us, tell us all about it," said his brother and sister.

"Come with me!" said the blue bird.

And they flew high, and they
flew low.
They flew here, and they
flew there. They flew
everywhere . . . all together.

1 Why didn't the little blue bird want to fly?

2 What happened in the story to make him fly?

3 What do you think the little blue bird saw when he was flying with the other birds?

4 Tell the story in your own words.

5 What other stories have you read that were about learning something new?

Write a Note to the Little Blue Bird

Think of something you just learned.
Write a short note to the little blue bird.
Tell him what you just learned to do!

Dear little blue bird,
I just learned how to ride a bike!
I'm glad you can fly!
Love, your friend Millie

Make a Bird Mural

There are many different kinds of birds.
Think of a bird you would like to draw.
Draw and color your bird.
Then cut it out.
Tape it on the bird mural.
Write its name.

cardinal

bluebird

chickadee

parrot

Find Out More

Find out about birds that
make good pets.

Library Computer

Search by:
1. title
2. author
3. subject

You can use a computer to find a book at the library.

Look at the Computer Screen

1 If you want to find books about birds, where would you put the pointer?

2 If you want to find the book *Where the Wild Things Are*, where would you put the pointer?

Where Did the Clothing Go?

A long time ago, there was a little purple bird.
He liked to move people's laundry.
He took clothes from one clothesline.
He put them on the next.

Ask yourself, "Why is this story make-believe?"

One night, a girl tried to catch the bird.
She hid in a clothesbasket.
Soon, the bird flew up to the clothesline.
The girl jumped out of the basket and threw a big net over the bird.
The scared bird said he was sorry for his tricks.
The girl believed the bird and let him go.
The town has not had mixed-up laundry since.

We know that this story is make-believe because —

○ people do not have laundry
○ birds do not steal laundry

Up in the Sky

When you fly in a plane, you look down
And see houses around a small town.
Cars and trucks look like toys on a rug.
Big brown cows look like little brown bugs.
The only sound that you can hear
Is the noise of the engine in your ears.
It's a joy to be buzzing around—
Thousands and thousands of feet
    off the ground!

Meet Susan Alcott

Susan Alcott began her career as a children's book editor. Then she started writing children's books. Alcott especially likes writing biographies. "It's a great way to meet history's most fascinating people," she says.

Meet Stacey Schuett

Stacey Schuett gets her ideas from family, friends, and the things around her. She really likes to draw animals. "You don't have to be perfect to be an artist. If you like art, just stick with it," Schuett says.

Young Amelia Earhart
A Dream to Fly

by Susan Alcott

illustrated by Stacey Schuett

Amelia Earhart was America's
greatest woman pilot. Her daring
adventures made her famous all
over the world.

Amelia was born in Kansas in 1897.
In those days, girls had to act like ladies.
They could not play games like boys did.

But Amelia and her younger sister Muriel were lucky. Their mother and father believed girls and boys should be treated the same.

Amelia and Muriel were allowed to play baseball, football, and other sports. Amelia loved to think of exciting games to play.

One winter day Amelia, Muriel, and their friends went sledding. But just as Amelia was zooming down a big hill, a large, horse-drawn wagon crossed the street in front of her.

The driver did not see Amelia. And there was no time for Amelia to stop. But Amelia was calm. She steered the sled *underneath* the horse!

Amelia saw her first airplane at the Iowa State Fair when she was 11 years old. She did not know then that one day airplanes would change her life.

269

When Amelia grew up, she worked as a nurse.
One day Amelia and a friend saw some pilots
doing tricks in the air. As she watched the planes
turn and dive, Amelia got very excited.

"I must learn to fly," Amelia said. And so she began taking lessons.

Amelia learned everything about planes.
She could even take an engine apart and
put it back together!

Amelia learned how to fly in all kinds
of weather. Her teacher taught her to
fly at night, too.

Finally, after practicing for a long time, Amelia got her pilot's license. She was 25 years old.

Soon Amelia became the greatest woman pilot in the world.

In 1932, Amelia flew across
the Atlantic Ocean by herself.
No woman had ever done that.

Amelia set many records in her little plane.
People all over the world cheered her on.

DAILY RECORD
AMELIA SETS NEW RECORD

In 1937, Amelia decided to do something no one had ever done before. She wanted to fly around the world.

She and a man named
Fred Noonan began their
around-the-world adventure
in Miami, Florida.

For a month, everything went well. Then Amelia and Fred headed for Howland Island in the Pacific Ocean.

But something went wrong. Amelia and Fred
never arrived at Howland Island. And no one
ever heard from them again.

No one knows what happened
to Amelia Earhart. Most people think
her plane crashed in the ocean.

But Amelia has never been forgotten. Her
brave spirit and exciting adventures still
inspire people today.

289

READ TOGETHER

Story Questions & Activities

1. How did Amelia keep from getting hurt by the horse?

2. What is a pilot's license?

3. If you had a broken toy, do you think Amelia could have fixed it? Why or why not?

4. Tell about the important parts of Amelia Earhart's life.

5. Who was braver: Johnny Appleseed or Amelia Earhart? Why?

Write About You

Write a newspaper article about your life.

Tell when and where you were born.

Tell about growing up.

My Life

I was born in San Antonio. I was born on November 12, 1992. I live in a blue house with my mom, dad, and little sister.

290

Make a "Me" Collage

Draw a picture of yourself.
Add pictures of things you like.
Use paper, photos, and crayons.

Find Out More

Find out more about airplanes
and other things that fly.
Find out some of their names
and what they are used for.

Glossary

A glossary tells us what words mean.
Words in a glossary are in ABC order.

actor An actor is someone who acts in a play or movie.

adult An adult is a grownup like your parents.

airplane An airplane is a machine that flies.

animal An animal is a living thing such as a pig, a cat, or a dog.

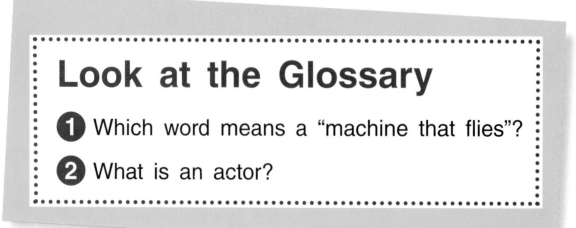

Look at the Glossary

1 Which word means a "machine that flies"?

2 What is an actor?

What Does Steven Do?

Steven is a silly snail
whose shell is green and black.
He leaves a messy trail when
he slides along the path.

Steven is a silly snail
who slides from here to there.
He spends his day out in the sun
and does not have a care.

Which is the best summary of this story?

○ Steven spends his days in the sun.

○ Steven spends his days eating plants.

A summary tells the story again in one sentence.

Going Places

Beep! Beep! Toot! Toot!
Choose the way to go.
Plane, boat, bus, and car.
We travel near. We travel far.
Turn left. Turn right.
Go up the hill and down.
Red light, green light.
Now we are in town.
One coin. Two coins.
Pay your fare today.
What joy! What fun!
We are traveling away.

TOW
AWAY
ZONE

TAXI

ONE
→
WAY

TIME

FOR KIDS

SPECIAL REPORT

On
the
Go!

Think! How would you get ten bags of food home from the store? Would you walk home? Would you ride in a car, a bus, or a train?

Today there are many ways to get from place to place. These are called transportation. There are three kinds. You can travel by land, water, or air. Let's find out more about each one.

Going by Land

Long before we had cars, people had to carry things. They used horses to help them.

Today, you can get to places by car, bus, or train. There is a kind of train that goes underground. It is called a subway. The subway is a fast way to go places. You may decide to go on the subway if you are in a rush.

Trucks are also used to move things by land. There are a lot of trucks on the roads. There are small pickup trucks and big trucks with many wheels. How many trucks have you seen today?

FIND OUT MORE

Visit our website:
www.mhschool.com/reading

*inter***NET**
CONNECTION

A story from the editors of *TIME FOR KIDS*.

Going by Water

Ships and boats are used to move people and things by water. Many cities have busy ports. Ports are places where things get put on and taken off ships. Have you ever been on a ship?

Going by Air

Airplanes move people and things very quickly. You can fly across the country in less than five hours! Do you know how long that would take by car?

Transportation helps keep us all moving. What is your favorite way to go from place to place?

Story Questions & Activities

 1 What does *transportation* mean?

2 What kinds of transportation that you have read about have wheels?

3 Is there a way you can get around on wheels?

4 Tell about "On the Go!" in your own words.

5 By what form of transportation do you think the package for Silvia arrived?

Write about Transportation

Choose a way of transportation that you like from the story. Describe how you would use this way to travel.

Make a Maze

Use paper. Write **Start** at one end. Draw a car, bus, train, or plane next to **Start**. At the other end of the paper, write **Finish**. Draw a place you want to visit over **Finish**. Draw some roads or paths. Ask a friend to follow a path to get from **Start** to **Finish**.

ZOO

Finish

Start

Find Out More

Find out about a helicopter.
In what ways can it help you?

Look It Up!

People have many ways of getting information.

book   **dictionary**

tape

Look at the Pictures

1 What can you use to help you learn more about subways?

2 What can you use to listen to the tune of a new song?

Transportation

There are different ways to get to places.
You can walk or ride a bike for short trips.
You can drive a car for longer trips.

Trains are easy to take.
Planes are easy, too.
Planes can cross over seas and oceans.
Trains cannot.
Planes also move faster than trains.
How do you get from here to there?

Only one answer fits the story best.

Different kinds of transportation —
○ are good for different kinds of trips
○ make it difficult to get from here to there

304

My Mami Takes Me To The Bakery

Let's buy pan de agua, daughter.
Pan is bread and agua, water.
Good fresh bread of flour and water.
Good fresh pan de agua, daughter.

Inside the panadería,
There's the hot sweet smell of pan.
Good day, says the plump panadero.
(The baker's a very nice man.)

How many loaves, Señora, he asks:
Uno . . . dos?
Dos? Sí, sí.
Two, por favor, says my mami.
Two loaves for my daughter and me.

by Charlotte Pomerantz

Glossary

This glossary can help you to find out the meanings of words in this book that you may not know.

The words are listed in alphabetical order. There is a simple sentence for each word. Sometimes a picture illustrating the word is also included.

Sample Entry

Letter

Main Entry

Sample Sentence

Little

That bug is very **little.**

Another word for **little** is *small.*

Sample Picture

Aa

Airplanes

Go on an **airplane** if you want to go far away.

Amelia

Amelia Earhart was the first woman to fly an airplane across the Atlantic Ocean.

Animals

These **animals** live in the jungle.

Bb

Bear

My stuffed **bear** is big and brown.

Beautiful

The sky is **beautiful.**

Another word for **beautiful** is *pretty.*

Bird

Look at that **bird** fly.

Blue

Lan's favorite color is **blue.**

Bugs

The **bugs** are black.

Cc

Clouds

You can see many **clouds** in the sky.

Dd

Disappear(s)(ed)

A magician makes things **disappear.**

Ff

Flew

The plane **flew** away.

Friend

Invite your **friend** over to play.

Another word for **friend** is *buddy.*

Gg

Goat

A **goat** is an animal that lives on a farm.

Hh

Horse

The **horse** lives in the barn.

Ii

Iowa

I live in the state of **Iowa.**

Ll

Little

That bug is very **little.**

Another word for **little** is *small.*

311

Mm

Mira

Mira means *look* in Spanish.

Mother

His **mother** walks him to school.

Mouse

The **mouse** likes to eat cheese.

Nn

Nerves

Nerves tell your brain what to do.

Night

We go to sleep at **night.**

Nothing

I have **nothing** to do today.

Ocean

Whales live in the **ocean.**

Owl

An **owl** is a bird that is awake at night.

Pp

Pajamas

You wear **pajamas** when you sleep.

Pizza

We had **pizza** for lunch.

Rr

Rosita

Rosita sent a package to Silvia.

Ss

Sense

Your **sense** of touch helps you know how things feel.

Shoes

I got fancy red **shoes** for my birthday.

Silvia

This is **Silvia** from *New Shoes for Silvia.*

Squirrel

The **squirrel** will eat that nut.

Subway

We take the **subway** to our house.

Tía

Tía means "aunt" in Spanish.

315

Tiny

A ladybug is a **tiny** insect.

Another word for **tiny** is *small.*

Train

The **train** is going very fast.

Transportation

People need to use some sort of **transportation** to get around.

Trucks

These **trucks** carry food to the stores.

Vibrations

You feel **vibrations** when a big truck zooms past.

Water

Your plants need **water** to grow.

Wheels

The **wheels** on the bike can go fast or slow.

Wings

Birds use their **wings** to fly.

Wood

Put more **wood** on the fire.

World

The **world** is full of people.

INDEX OF AUTHORS AND ILLUSTRATORS

INDEX OF STORIES

ACKNOWLEDGMENTS

The publisher gratefully acknowledges permission to reprint the following copyrighted material:

"Baby Chick" by Aileen Fisher from RUNNY DAYS, SUNNY DAYS. Copyright © 1958 by Aileen Fisher, © renewed 1986. Originally published by Abelard-Schuman, NY. Used by permission of Marian Reiner for the author.

"A Friend for Little Bear" by Harry Horse. Copyright © 1996 by Harry Horse. Reprinted by permission of Candlewick Press Inc., Cambridge, MA.

"My Mami Takes Me to The Bakery" by Charlotte Pomerantz from THE TAMARINDO PUPPY AND OTHER POEMS. Text copyright © 1980 by Charlotte Pomerantz. Illustrations copyright © 1980 by Byron Barton. Reprinted by permission of Greenwillow Books.

Entire text, art, and cover of "New Shoes for Silvia" by Johanna Hurwitz. Illustrated by Jerry Pinkney. Text copyright © 1993 by Johanna Hurwitz. Illustrations copyright © 1993 by Jerry Pinkney. By permission of Morrow Junior Books, a division of William Morrow and Company, Inc.

"Owl and the Moon" from OWL AT HOME by Arnold Lobel. Copyright © 1975 by Arnold Lobel. Reprinted by permission of HarperTrophy®, A Division of HarperCollins Publishers.

"Seven Sillies" by Joyce Dunbar, illustrated by Chris Downing. Text copyright © 1993 by Joyce Dunbar. Illustrations copyright © by Chris Downing. First published by Anderson Press, London. All rights reserved.

"Shrinking Mouse" by Pat Hutchins. Copyright © 1997 by Pat Hutchins. Reprinted by permission of Greenwillow Books.

"Solution" by Leland B. Jacobs. Reprinted by permission.

"The Story of a Blue Bird" by Tomek Bogacki. Copyright © 1998 by Tomek Bogacki. Reprinted by permission of Frances Foster Books, Farrar Straus & Giroux.

"You Can't Smell a Flower with Your Ear!" written by Joanna Cole, illustrated by Mavis Smith. Text copyright © 1994 by Joanna Cole. Illustrations copyright © 1994 by Mavis Smith. Published by arrangement with Penguin Putnam Books for Young Readers, a division of Penguin Putnam, Inc.

"Young Amelia Earhart" by Susan Alcott, illustrated by James Anton. Copyright © 1992 by Troll Associates. Reprinted by permission of Troll Associates.

Illustration
Kevin Hawkes, 8–9; Richard Hull, 10–11; Chris Downing, 12–41, 42tl, 42cr, 43; Daniel Del Valle, 42b, 78br, 79, 114b, 116, 139; Eldon Doty, 45, 141, 151; Annie Lunsford, 46–47; Pat Hutchins, 48–77, 78tl, 80; Ken Bowser, 81; Michael Grejniec, 82–83; Mavis Smith, 84–113, 114tr, 115bl; Nancy Freeman, 118–119; Doug Roy, 115t; Bernard Adnet, 117; Arnold Lobel, 120–138; Krystyna Stasiak, 142–143; Alexi Natchev, 152–153; Jennifer Rarey, 154–155; Kim Fernandez, 156–157; Harry Horse, 158–187, 188tl; Daniel Del Valle, 188br, 222bl, 223cr, 255t, 292tr; Rita Lascaro, 190, 292; Bernard Adnet, 191, 293; DyAnne Di Salvo–Ryan, 192–193; Jerry Pinkney, 194–221, 222 cr; Eldon Doty, 225; Helen Ward, 226–227; Tomek Bogacki, 228–254, 255bl; Ken Bowser, 257, 303; Michael Letzig, 258–259; Stacey Schuett, 260–289, 290l; Doug Roy, 294–295; Nancy Tobin, 301–302; Mike Cressy, 304–305; John Carozza, 308, 311; Felipe Galindo, 314; Miles Parnell, 312.

Photography
12: b.r. Courtesy of Andersen Press. t.l. Courtesy of Andersen Press; 48: b.l. (c) 1990 Casual Candid. t.l. Courtesy of Laurence Hutchins; 84: t. Courtesy of Joanna Cole. 120: t. Ian Anderson. 158: (c) 1998 Murdo McCloud. 228: t. 260: b. Courtesy of Stacey Shuett. 309: Uniphoto/Andre Jenny. 310: George Hall Photography. 311: Liaison International/Ed Lallo. 313: b. The Stock Market/Jay Schlegel. 315: The Stock Market/Alan Schein. 316: The Stock Market/Kunio Owaki. 317: Liaison International/(c) Sam Sargent.